ABC's of Dating

Wishing you Dating & Relationship success!

- Katherin

ABC's OF DATING: Simple Strategies for Dating Success!

Copyright © 2009 by Katherin Scott

All rights reserved. Reproduction and distribution are forbidden. No part of this publication may be reproduced, stored in a retrieval system, or transmitted by any other means, electronic, mechanical, photocopying, recording, or otherwise, without written permission from the author. Please contact CoachKatherin@yahoo.com.

The author and publisher have used their best efforts in preparing this book and shall in no event be held liable for any loss or damages including but not limited to special, incidental, or consequential.

ISBN-13: 978-0-578-00748-9
ISBN-10: 0578007487

Cover design and inside text design/layout by Katherin Scott.

Published by Macro Connections Publishing, a DBA of Macro Connections, LLC.

ABC's of Dating

Simple Strategies for Dating Success!

Katherin Scott, M.A.

The Dating Coach

ABC's OF DATING: Simple Strategies for Dating Success!

TABLE OF CONTENTS

Author's Note	vi
A is for **A**vailability	1
B is for **B**alance	9
C is for **C**larity	12
D is for First **D**ate Conversations	17
E is for **E**nergy	20
F is for **F**inding Mr. or Ms. Right	26
G is for **G**et Flirtatious	34
H is for **H**ealing	39
I is for **I**ntimacy	43
J is for **J**ust Do It!	49
K is for **K**indness	52
L is for **L**istening	55
M is for **M**aturity	58
N is for **N**on-Negotiables	62

ABC's OF DATING: Simple Strategies for Dating Success!

O is for **O**wning Your **O**wn Issues	66
P is for **P**ositive Mental Attitude	69
Q is for **Q**uit It!	74
R is for **R**omantic **R**ejection	80
S is for **S**uccessful **S**ingle	84
T is for **T**ell **T**he **T**ruth	87
U is for **U**nderstanding	92
V is for Dating **V**enues	100
W is for **W**illingness to **W**ork	104
X is for e**X**it	107
Y is for **Y**ou	111
Z is for **Z**oos	118
Afterward	125
About the Author	126

[v]

ABC's OF DATING: Simple Strategies for Dating Success!

Author's Note

I wrote this ABC book for singles and for all stages of the dating process.

My intention is also to share valuable information to assist you to grow your relationship once you find that *someone special*.

Some say it's easy to fall in love. That may or may not be true for you. Either way, I believe the next step - to keep that love alive for both partners – is crucial, so I've included valuable information on how to deepen the love.

The ABC's of Dating provides simple, specific strategies for dating success. These strategies are simple *and significant* for finding lasting love. That was intentional on my part, as I want you to understand that finding love isn't hard – when you know the strategies.

This book may be read chapter by chapter, A to Z, or feel free to skip around and read each chapter randomly - whatever topic catches your attention in the moment.

Read a chapter, do the exercise, practice what you learned, and then reflect on what it means *for you*.

You may want to read one chapter every day for a 26-day transformational month or focus on one chapter each week for six life-changing months.

The choice is yours.

Each chapter ends with an exercise and a time for reflection. I invite you to be diligent to complete each one.

Doing the work *is* the shortcut to finding love!

Do not be fooled. Too many people believe love will magically happen if they just want it deeply enough.

Like the final step in the Law of Attraction, unless you actually **take action** – nothing will manifest for you.

You deserve all that life has to offer, including a loving relationship. Take the time for yourself, do the work and find the love of your dreams.

I wish you Happy Dating - and much Love!

-Katherin

> *"For it was not into my ear you whispered but into my heart. It was not my lips you kissed, but my soul."*
>
> *~Judy Garland*

ABC's OF DATING: Simple Strategies for Dating Success!

 is for AVAILABILITY

"Desire is proof of availability." ~Robert Collier

Are you truly available to date? How can you tell?

People date for four reasons; friendship, social connection, sex, or to find a long-term partner.

If you're on your quest to find your life partner, you need to be truly *single, ready and available.*

That sounds like common sense, doesn't it? But it's not. Too many people are looking for a life partner long before they're ready.

Let's start with the idea of being single.

> *If you're separated, you should either be working on your marriage or on your divorce – not dating!*
>
> **- Coach Katherin**

If you're separated from your spouse, whether legally separated or not – you're still married! People who are separated need to be working on their marriage or their divorce, not dating. Dating is a distraction from the business at hand and only confuses the issues.

If your purpose for dating is for friendship or social connection and not to find the love of your life at the present time, no problem.

Just be sure of your intention and be clear to those you're dating. Be up-front about your purpose and do not lead anyone into thinking you're looking for a life partner if you're not.

And, if you're dating just for sex, again, be very clear to those you're dating about your purpose. Go out and have sex – safe sex. However, don't fool yourself into thinking your sex partner will turn into your life partner. It rarely happens.

> *If you're "touch starved" get a massage instead of jumping into bed with the first person who shows interest in you.*
>
> *- Coach Katherin*

On the other hand, if you're feeling drawn to have sex because you're "touch starved," I recommend you get regular massages rather than jumping into bed with the first person who shows interest in you. Monthly massages at a minimum. A weekly massage is imperative if you haven't experienced healthy touch in a while.

So how can you be sure about your dating availability and readiness?

Take a few minutes to answer the 10 questions in the Dating Availability Assessment and find out if you are truly ready for the life and love you desire.

> "Vision is the spectacular that inspires us to carry out the mundane."
>
> ~Chris Widener

ABC's OF DATING: Simple Strategies for Dating Success!

Dating Availability Assessment

> **Rating Scale:**
>
> *Honestly rate each of the following on a scale of 0 to 10.*
>
> **8-10: Good;** I feel confident this area of my life is strong.
> **5-7: Satisfactory;** This area needs work but most likely would not sabotage my future relationship.
> **0-4: Needs Improvement;** I am concerned about this area of my life.

Question:	Score
1. I know what I want. I have a clear vision for my life and my relationship requirements, needs and wants.	
2. I know who I am. I have a clear understanding of my strengths and weaknesses and a defined plan for continual personal growth.	
3. I have narrowed the gaps between *who I am* and *what I want* so that I do not need to be "rescued" or "completed" by a partner.	

4. I know my "Must-Have's." I have a written list of at lease 5 non-negotiable requirements that must be present in my relationship with a partner.

5. I have clear conversational questions to quickly pre-qualify or dis-qualify a potential partner. These questions are conversational in nature, not interrogative or intrusive, and allow me to promptly screen a potential partner based on my "must-have's."

6. I am happy and successful being single. My life is full and satisfying and I have not put my life on hold waiting for a relationship to happen. I realize my purpose for finding a life partner is to add value to my life, not to "complete" it.

7. I am ready and available for commitment and do not have any legal, financial or emotional issues that would negatively affect my availability for a partner.

8. My career / work are satisfying. My work is enjoyable, supports my financial needs and would not interfere with my relationship with a partner.	
9. I have effective dating and relationship skills. I am comfortable initiating contact with potential partners and disengaging for others who are not a match for me. I maintain healthy boundaries, both physical and emotional, allow myself to be appropriately vulnerable with others, and am aware of and have dealt with my past relationship issues.	
10. I have effective communication skills. I know how to clearly express my needs and wants and courageously communicate with others, even in times of stress / conflict. I practice active listening and am aware of other's facial expressions and nonverbal behavior.	
TOTAL:	

Results:

76-100:   GREEN LIGHT
You are ready and available and well on you way to achieving the life and love you desire.

50-75:   YELLOW LIGHT
Use caution before committing to a partner. Take time to work on those areas needed to improve your readiness.

0-49:   RED LIGHT
Take a break from seeking a life partner. Focus on becoming more successful and happy in your life and available for a relationship.

What are your strongest areas?

What areas need improvement?

What do you need to learn more about?

What area from the Dating Availability Assessment could most interfere with the success of your next relationship?

What exactly do you need to do / know / learn in order to improve your dating availability?

MY ACTION PLAN for AVAILABILITY:

 is for BALANCE

"Happiness is not a matter of intensity but of balance, order, rhythm and harmony."
~Thomas Merton

Is your life in balance?

The expression "work / life balance" was first used in the late 1970's to describe the balance between a person's work and personal life. However, the idea of a balanced life is so much more than that.

Where do you actually spend you time?

How much of your work is invading your personal life?

And, how much of your personal life is affected by the stress of trying to balance all the many responsibilities in your life?

Also, do you use the amount of time you spend at work as an excuse for not having time to date?

If you're truly looking to find your life partner, you must strike a balance in your life which includes time for dating.

ABC's OF DATING: Simple Strategies for Dating Success!

Learn to Strike a Balance

Here are ideas to help you find a balance that best fits you *and* includes time for dating:

1. Keep a log. For one week, track how you spend your time. Keep track of work time, personal time, activities, chores, time spent dating, etc. It's important to understand where your time is actually spent. Eliminate as many unnecessary tasks as possible.

2. Learn to say NO. Do not take on any additional tasks unless you let go of something currently on your plate. Say "NO" to meaningless tasks and say "YES" to yourself, your goals and dreams.

3. Leave work at work. Do not allow your work to creep into your personal time and space. Honestly assess if you're working too much because you're lonely.

4. Nurture yourself. Set aside time each day for sleeping, exercising and activities which rejuvenate you. Practice stress management techniques.

5. Organize your chores. Schedule most of you routine chores for workdays so they don't consume your only free days.

6. Set aside [at least] one day / night each week for dating. Plan a fun night out, spend time online dating, or get together with a singles group for a fun activity.

> "Women need real moments of solitude and self-reflection to balance out how much of ourselves we give away."
>
> ~Barbara De Angelis

Remember, creating balance in your life is not a one-time activity. It's an ongoing process.

Learn to simplify your life, prioritize effectively, set and keep boundaries and remove unnecessary tasks.

MY ACTION PLAN for BALANCE:

is for CLARITY

"More important for the quest for certainty is the quest for clarity." – Francois Gautier

As a dating coach, I've heard this question over and over from singles, men and women alike; "Can you help me find a life partner?"

My response is always the same, "Sure. What qualities and characteristics are important to you in a mate?"

At this point, I usually get a blank stare, as though this is the first time in their single life they've ever even *begun* to think about this important question.

How about you? Would you be able to quickly list the key characteristics and values you are looking for in a partner?

It's my experience that men spend a lot of time thinking about the perfect car. Women spend a lot of time thinking about the perfect shoes or outfit.

But who spends time thinking about the perfect mate?

> *"People shop for a bathing suit with more care than they do a husband or wife."*
>
> *~Erma Bombeck*

Okay, what *are* some of the key characteristics you're looking for in a partner and what is a good way to evaluate a relationship for its long-term potential within the first few dates?

Here are six key areas to assess a potential partner early in the dating process (within 3-5 dates):

1. Mutual Respect:
Respect is crucial in any relationship, particularly in a life partnership or marriage. The litmus test for respect is determining if you want to emulate this person. What qualities do you respect in this person? Would you be happy if your child turns out like him/her?

2. Appreciate Your Differences:
Most people choose friends who are very similar to themselves. Not necessarily so with mates. It's those differences that make us crazy for a particular person in the first place then exactly what *drives* us crazy about them later.

Ask yourself this question, "If his/her personality and habits stay exactly the same as they are today, will I be happy 20, 30, 40+ years from now?"

If you can't be happy with the person the way he or she is now, stop dating them. Don't expect to change another person. You'll be frustrated and he/she will be resentful.

3. Alignment of Purpose:
Ask yourself, "Do we share common goals and priorities?"

Make sure you share the deeper level of connection that comes through sharing life's goals. Do you both want the same things out of life with regard to family, lifestyle, work, fun, relationships?

To avoid growing apart from your life partner, figure out what you're living for while you're single and then find someone who independently came to the same conclusion as you.

4. Chemistry:
Ask yourself, "Do I feel a sexual attraction, an excitement for this person? Have I fantasized about this person in a sexual manner?"

Men should be attracted to a woman early in the dating process.

Women may take longer to realize attraction and grow the chemistry. If a woman isn't feeling an attraction for a man within the first 3-5 dates, I suggest she ask herself a different question, namely, "Can I ever imagine myself kissing this man?"

If the answer is "yes", it's a possible match. If the answer is "no", stop dating and move on.

5. Intelligence:
Do you have a lot to talk about when you spend time together? Do you respect each other's way of thinking? Does he/she match your expectations regarding street smarts or book smarts?

6. Emotional Connection:
Men want a woman to trust him, accept and appreciate him. If you're a man, do you feel these things from her?

Women want to feel cared for, understood and respected. When you're with him, do you feel these?

In addition, if you feel listened to, valued, comfortable with the other person and also excited to spend time together, that's a sure sign of emotional connection.

If not, then it's a good time to re-evaluate your motives for the relationship.

~~~

3-5 dates may not seem long enough to evaluate a potential partner. However, it usually is. If you think you need more time to decide, date for no more than three months before revisiting the six keys above.

Then be honest. If the relationship doesn't muster up to the six keys, end the relationship. Simply let them know you don't believe they're a good match for you.

However, if you truly believe they match the qualities you're looking for – go for it and enjoy!

> "There is nothing as mysterious as something clearly seen."
>
> ~Robert Frost

MY ACTION PLAN for CLARITY:

ABC's OF DATING: Simple Strategies for Dating Success!

D is for FIRST DATE

CONVERSATIONS

"Conversation should touch everything, but should concentrate itself on nothing."
~Oscar Wilde

I believe first dates should be simple and short. No lengthy four course dinners. Just meet for coffee / tea. Meet in a public coffee shop or café. Any time of the day is fine.

Arrange to meet for about 30 – 60 minutes. Keeping additional time open is nice, in case you really hit it off, but unnecessary. It's best to have a great first date then schedule time to meet again if you really like each other.

> *"My grandmother's 90. She's dating. He's about 93. It's going great. They never argue. They can't hear each other."*
>
> *~Catherine Ladman*

What will you talk about? The First Date Conversation can make you or break you. Are you prepared? Here are some guidelines:

#1: Ask questions.
A good first date conversation is one in which you make your date feel special. Think of questions that are insightful, but not too personal. "What do you do for fun?" "Do you like to travel?" Both are good for starters.

#2: Don't dominate.
You can talk about work, you can talk about hobbies, or you can talk about travel—just don't do all the talking. The first date is not a time to give your resume. It's the time to show interest in your date. Ask questions that will get your date talking and listen, listen, listen. Just be sure to add something relevant from your own life from time to time.

#3: Think of a list of topics.
It's helpful to come prepared with possible questions. Good conversation topics are; work, hobbies, friends, travel, siblings, school, goals, food and drink preferences, movies, music and books.

#4: Don't be dogged.
Be responsive to your date's body language. Does she like talking about her work, or is it depressing? Aim for a topic that's interesting and makes her happy. A little bit of vulnerability or honesty can be good ("What are you passionate about?") but nothing that brings up too much unhappiness ("Why do you hate your parents?").

#5: Don't rush through the list of topics.

You're not taking a survey. The point of questions is to get a conversation going. If you've asked him about his work and he seems happy to keep talking about it, let him. Ask more questions about work. "You design dog kennels? That sounds interesting. How did you get into that?"

#6: Don't talk about exes.

Bringing up an ex may seem an excellent way to open that vulnerable side on the way to romance. It's not. The very mention of an ex is bad news and can cause the date to deteriorate fast. You're starting on a clean slate. Keep it clean.

And remember, it's just a conversation. You have them all the time. No need to enlist your friends in mock-date conversations full of insightful and responsive questions. Just relax, be yourself and have fun.

MY ACTION PLAN for FIRST DATE CONVERSATIONS:

ABC's OF DATING: Simple Strategies for Dating Success!

 is for ENERGY

"Passion is energy. Feel the power that comes from focusing on what excites you."
~Oprah Winfrey

What if I told you that you can attract love into your life just by changing the energy in your bedroom? Does that sound too "woo-woo" for you?

You can. And it's easier than you might think with feng shui.

Many people in our Western culture today have already been exposed to the traditions and practices of feng shui.

If you're well practiced in feng shui or even if feng shui is totally new to you, as you read this chapter, you will learn **simple, yet significant strategies to attract more love, romance, affection and sex into your life!**

Feng shui is the ancient Chinese art and science of placement. Feng shui, (pronounced FUNG SHWAY), is the Chinese term that literally means "Wind and Water."

By applying the principles of feng shui to the placement of objects in our environment, especially in our bedroom, we can balance the Chi (positive energy) and

[20]

correct the flow of energy, attract a new love relationship and/or improve an existing one.

Although the name Feng Shui often seems strange and foreign to people in Western cultures, feng shui is actually a very practical collection of principles and action steps that make good sense, both from a design perspective and from a holistic point of view.

> "Feng Shui is one-third common sense, one-third good design; the last third consists of ancient knowledge and traditions, enhancements and cures that may seem odd to us – but they work!"
>
> ~Unknown

Here are eight simple strategies you can apply to dramatically improve your love life:

1. The Position of Your Bed *Does* Matter
Ideally, a bed should be positioned on the wall diagonal from the door, but not directly in line with the door. This allows the occupant the widest possible view of the bedroom and anyone entering the space.

If for some reason the bed cannot be positioned here, hang a mirror so you can see the door clearly while lying in bed.

There should be equal distance on either side of the bed, to allow for a partner in the relationship. If the bed is pushed up against a wall, this may close off the flow of a partner into your life, or dis-empower an existing one.

This may also diminish the amount of sex in your relationship, because of the "closed-off" space. (However, this may be recommended for teenagers who live in your home.☺)

2. Remove Clutter Now!
Most people don't realize how profoundly clutter affects them. Removing clutter from your bedroom allows the Chi to flow in the space.

Remove anything that doesn't belong in the bedroom.

Remove everything from under your bed. Stashing junk under your bed will affect the quality of your sleep.

The added benefit is that lots of things will now have an opportunity to flow into your life when you make room for it.

3. Banish Past Love Relationships
Remove anything that reminds you of past – especially love gone bad – relationships. Gifts, pictures, sheets (it's especially important to purchase new sheets – 100% cotton, no polyester in them), anything that reminds you of a past romance should be removed from the bedroom, discarded or given to charity.

One woman I met actually had shoeboxes in her bedroom closet with labels of each past boyfriend's name on the front. Inside were mementos, pictures and letters given to her by the man and things that reminded her of him.

Once she realized the significance of hanging onto these past items, she removed them from her bedroom and created space for a wonderful new man to enter her life – which happened soon after!

4. Allow Chi to Enter and Circulate

Does your bedroom door open fully, or is it blocked? Check your front door too. Both should open wide to allow Chi to enter freely.

When you walk through your bedroom door, what is the first thing you see? Make it inviting and inspirational; a picture that inspires you, a round mirror which symbolizes completion and unity, fresh flowers, whatever makes you feel uplifted or reminds you of love and partnership.

Also, be sure to fix or replace anything that is broken in your bedroom. Change-out all burnt-out light bulbs, fix loose door knobs, remove dead plants and repaint over the marks on the walls.

5. Your Bedroom Is For Sleeping & Love

Your bedroom is not for working out or surfing the internet. Do not store exercise equipment or a computer in your bedroom. This can make a relationship seem like hard work or exertion.

6. Let Love In

Clean your closets and drawers to allow space for a love partner to come in.

If all of your space is filled to overflowing, nothing new can flow into your life – including that special someone.

Your goal is to free-up 20 - 25 percent of the space. And while you are at it, clean out your junk drawers too. Even if those bedroom drawers do close, if what's in them is unused and not needed, this can cause chaos in your love life.

7. Add Romance Generously
Bring romance into your bedroom with pairs of things; two candles, two matching (in size and weight) nightstands, two lamps – one on either side of the bed.

Bring in heart-shaped items, things that represent love to you or anything pink or red to symbolize love.

Be sure to pay attention to the scents in your room too. Bring in aromatherapy candles or incense to spice up the air.

8. Get Clear
Spend time visualizing your life partner and how wonderful your life will be with them in it. Add lots of detail to your daydreaming.

What will you be doing together? Where will you go? What will you see and experience? How will you spend your time together?

Collect pictures which remind you of love and happy times together. Write down your dreams or affirmations for a love partner and place those under your mattress.

~~~

By following these eight simple strategies and principles of feng shui, you will focus more clearly on the love, romance, affection and sex you want in your life. Notice how quickly things now flow into your life.

One last tip: during a full moon, go outside and blow bubbles to the sky to bring more love into your life. It may seem silly but the Universe will understand what you want and deliver more love to you. Just wait and see!

MY ACTION PLAN for ENERGY:

F is for FINDING Mr. or Ms. RIGHT

"Hi, I'm Mr. Right. Someone said you were looking for me."
~Austin Powers

Finding Mr. or Ms. Right seems to be on a lot of singles' minds these days. What if you've met someone whom you think might be "the one." How will you know if they are Mr. or Ms. Right for you?

> "My boyfriend used to ask his mother, 'How can I find the right woman for me?' and she would answer,
> 'Don't worry about finding the right woman – concentrate on becoming the right man.'"
>
> ~Unknown

Let's start with the ladies. Here are ten sure signs to know he is right for you.

#1: You don't think he's perfect—except for you.
If you think he *is* perfect, you have a problem. I don't even know your guy, but I know he's not perfect. If you think he is, you don't know him, or you're in denial.

Before you sign the dotted line, you need to know your guy—and know you can handle his imperfections. If you know him, think he's great, but know he's just a man, you may be on the right track.

#2: You like who you are with him.
If you're going to stick with someone forever, you'd better like not only him, but you.

How does he affect you? Do you feel more shy, more brazen, more something than you'd like when you're with him?

Or does he bring out the best parts of you? You should like what (or who) he brings out in you.

#3: He turns you on—and tucks you in.
With The One, you'll be equally comfortable in lacy lingerie and dirty sweats.

Your One and Only is the guy you can be most yourself with. That means all your selves, from the sexy lady in stilettos to the worn-out mom with stale milk on her shirt.

#4: He thinks he's lucky.
Never, ever settle on a man who doesn't think he's the luckiest man in the world. If he can't believe he's with *you*, you've got a good thing.

#5: You argue.
You need to know you can get mad at The One, and that you can work things out. With The One, you'll be able to be honest and have it build the relationship rather than weaken it.

You need to be able to talk things through and move on, together.

#6: You laugh.
He doesn't need to be funny, and neither do you. But if you don't tickle each other's funny bone, something's wrong.

The One is someone who makes life more fun just because he's there.

> "Men are respectable only as they respect."
>
> ~Ralph Waldo Emerson

#7: You respect him.
Maybe he's amazing in bed, maybe he makes you feel gorgeous, maybe he's rich as Donald Trump, but if you don't respect him, he's not your man.

#8: He thinks you're beautiful.
All the time. He thinks your eyes are beautiful, your legs, the small of your back. He tells you. He looks at you. He touches you.

He thinks you're beautiful with makeup and without, in your bathing suit and birthday suit, in cut-offs smeared with paint. He's proud you're his.

#9: You see him in your future.
Can you imagine raising children with him? Can you imagine him nursing you through cancer? Will he be kind to your mother when she's old? You should be able to imagine a future with him with excitement, not with fear.

> *"Without trust, words become the hollow sound of a wooden gong. With trust, words become life itself."*
>
> ~Unknown

#10: You trust him.
You can't be with a guy you don't trust. If he's The One, this is a guy you can trust implicitly, absolutely. This is a guy you can't even imagine cheating on you.

Finally, and most importantly of all, if he's Mr. Right, you love him—and he loves you.

> *"Don't settle for a relationship that won't let you be yourself."*
>
> ~Oprah Winfrey

And now, for the gentlemen. Here are ten ways to know for sure if she's Ms. Right for you!

#1: She's your equal.
Women aren't supposed to be ornaments anymore. You want to be with a woman who's as smart, capable, and independent as you.

You need to be able to count on her. If you have to baby her all the time in everything, you may be in a bad relationship.

#2: You trust her.
If she's The One, you'll be able to trust her. You can trust her to be faithful, to keep your secrets, and to keep her promises. You don't need to waste any time checking up on her.

#3: You can have reasonable, intelligent arguments.
If you're with a woman who shrieks or weeps every time you have a disagreement, you're not going to have a pleasant life.

A long-term partner is one you can work with - and that means you can argue with her without your relationship going to pieces.

> "Laugh a lot, and when you're older, all your wrinkles will be in the right places."
>
> ~Unknown

#4: You laugh together.
You're not playing the field now, so you don't need to be funny anymore. But you need to laugh. You and The One will have more fun with each other just because you're there.

If you don't make each other laugh, she may not be The One.

#5: You're a better man because of her.
This is the woman you'll spend the rest of your life with. Do you want to spend the rest of your life being some jerk you hate?

The love of your life will inspire and challenge you to the best you.

#6: She supports and respects you.
If she doesn't think the world of you, chances are she won't be happy long. And you won't be happy either.

#7: She supports and respects your dreams.
Life partners need to share their dreams. It's okay if you want to open a pizza parlor and she wants to be a lawyer. It's not okay if you will only live on a sailboat and she hates the water.

Strong partners compromise and work to please each other, but it's important that what you value in life, and want for your future, are similar things. She needs to be excited about your dreams, and you should be excited about hers.

#8: She knows you're not perfect.
She really knows you, and she's okay with that. She knows you yell at other drivers and that you sometimes miss the toilet seat.

She's comfortable with you, all the time, and you're comfortable with her.

#9: You know she's not perfect.
If you think your woman is a goddess, you may have not have gotten to know her yet. Yes, she really may be as shockingly gorgeous as you think she is. But she has faults. Do you know them? Can you live with them?

Sometimes the littlest things are the hardest in a relationship. Are you okay with the way she smacks her lips when she eats? You'd better be.

#10: You're proud to belong to her.
If you don't want to be seen with your woman or try to keep her apart from your friends, she's not The One. If this is a woman you should be with forever, you'll want people to know her. You'll be proud to be with her.

Of course, the most important sign is love. She's not Ms. Right unless you love her, and she loves you. A lot.

> "Lots of people want to ride with you in the limo, but what you want is someone who will take the bus with you when the limo breaks down."
>
> ~Oprah Winfrey

MY ACTION PLAN for FINDING MR. or MS. RIGHT:

G is for GET FLIRTATIOUS

"Yeah I flirt, I'm not blind and I'm not dead!"
~Dolly Parton

The art of flirting is the art of making someone else feel attractive—in a tasteful, understated way. Don't be too obvious. Don't be too subtle. See? It's simple.

Okay, let's break it down a little more.

> *"Flirting is the gentle art of making a man feel pleased with himself."*
>
> ~Helen Rowland

What exactly are the elements of the art of flirting?

#1: Eye contact.
Your first contact with someone attractive will probably be a glance, so eye contact is extremely important.

You can convey interest, confidence, and non-sleaziness all in a glance.

When you're letting someone know you like them, look into their eyes just a fraction longer than you normally would—then look away. Don't overwhelm the moment with emotional weight. But keep looking. Look back; look again; be caught gazing when they've looked away.

Show interest, but don't ogle.

There are some gender differences here. Women: you can be pretty obvious. Men: by "gazing," we mean gazing at a woman's face. If she catches you looking southward—particularly while she's talking to you—you may be done.

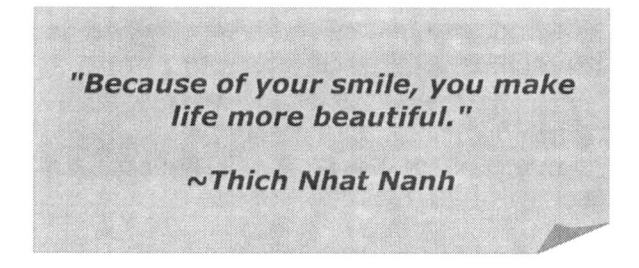

> "Because of your smile, you make life more beautiful."
>
> ~Thich Nhat Nanh

#2: Smile.
That's it. Smile a lot. Everyone likes smiling.

#3: Touch.
Careful! Establish interest before you move into this step. Men, especially, need to be careful. If you're subtle, touching can be extremely effective.

Men, brush hands. Touch her shoulder or her back when you get her a drink. Stand a touch closer than you normally would—but just a touch. Don't back her into a wall.

Women, you can be more obvious. You can touch his arm or his hands. Quietly touch your own face, your neck, and your legs. Subtly indicate your sexual interest is being aroused.

#4: Move your body.
You want to position your body so you communicate attraction. Lean forward when you're talking. Turn your body toward your interest. Mirror body posture.

#5: Talk.
You do not need an opening line. In fact, a bland, general comment can work better. You can show interest in a non-threatening, non-committal way. From there you can build on a mutual topic of interest.

Be sure to listen as much as you talk. Show a great deal of attention to what your interest has to say.

#6: Laugh.
Timing is important, of course, but in general laughter is attractive.

#7: Be funny.
Actually, being funny is not really necessary to flirting. You can be charming—as in, charm someone into feeling charming—without being witty, original, smart, or comedic.

But yes, like wild good looks, being funny helps. Of course, you have to be funny to the person you're talking to. Don't use a joke involving a dead animal if you're talking to a member of the Humane Society.

> "The greatest compliment that was ever paid me was when one asked me what I thought, and attended to my answer."
>
> ~Henry David Thoreau

#8: Compliment, compliment.
Again, tastefulness! "You have an excellent hiney" is not a great opener. It should not even be used thirty minutes into a conversation. It's good if you can come up with something at least somewhat original.

Complimenting eyes and smiles are safe choices, and they'll generally be welcome, but try to branch out in complimenting someone's clothes, ideas, or accomplishments. Don't go overboard.

> "Being nice is one of many bridges on the road to Happiness."
>
> ~Donna A. Favors

#9: Be nice.
Be positive when you talk, be friendly, and be courteous.

#10: Practice.
Flirting is like a muscle. Use it or lose it.

~~~

Social scientists will tell you a woman crosses her legs when she's sexually interested, and that men stand taller and lower their voices. Maybe that's true, but it's also true that flirting is not a science.

Be sensitive to your interest's signals. They may not align with your flirtation manual. Be flexible and change course as needed.

MY ACTION PLAN for GET FLIRTATIOUS:

H is for HEALING AFTER A BREAK-UP

"The greatest healing therapy is love."
~Hubert H. Humphrey

Dating is fun. What's not so fun is breaking-up.

Most of us have been through at least one break-up that was especially hard. We all get through it. My wish for you is to get through it well. By that I mean, be healed – truly healed.

Some of the time we hang on too long to a not-good-for-us person or to a bad relationship. Worse yet is to punish our *current* relationship for what someone did to us in our *previous* relationship.

Yes, it's hard when your loved one dumps you. But knowing how to move forward in a healthy way is imperative.

Perhaps out of guilt, or perhaps out of consideration, sometimes our I-just-dumped-you person says, "But we can be friends, can't we?"

Somehow muster the courage to say, "NO. We can't be friends. If this is the end, it is the end of everything."

Agreeing to "be friends" has a multitude of overtures. It will mean your ex feels better about dumping you, and it will most likely mean you are hoping to worm your way back into their life.

Know when a good thing is over.

If you want to heal as quickly as possible, make it a clean break.

To get the finality set in your mind, cut a shoelace or a piece of cloth into two pieces and stare at them. There they are. Two separate things. Totally divided.

If you want to heal quickly, that's how you must see it. A new day *WILL* come.

Go out of your way to avoid your ex, but if you do accidentally meet them, hold your head up high; look them straight in the eye and say, "Hi. You're looking well." Don't let them see the hurt. Wait for a short reply, and *move on, ignoring them for whatever time remains.*

Making a clean break means you must destroy the mementos you cherish. It may not be something you can do immediately, but for your own good, do it as soon as possible.

Pictures are the first things to go. News clippings and gifts are next. Everything that even slightly reminds you of your ex must go; jewelry, clothing, and objects. Make a clean break.

You will be grieving as you try to go through the motions of life, and that's normal. But, believe it or not, healing *will* eventually come.

Give yourself permission to go through the grieving process. It's important. Acknowledge that you lost more than a prospective mate. You lost your whole future.

You lost your dreams and ambitions. And equally important, you either lost your self-esteem and self-worth, or it's badly damaged.

Realize that the hardest thing about a break-up is not the loss of a partner, or the loss of companionship, or the fun times you had. The hardest part is the rejection.

Fortunately, it is also the easiest to correct.

The very first thing you should do after a break-up is FLIRT a little. No, your heart won't be in it, but there is a little actor in everyone. And when someone flirts back, you have just reaffirmed that you are still a desirable person; you are still attractive; you still have "the touch".

And you will be restored, bit by bit.

It's time to treat yourself in whatever way you would normally like. No, you won't enjoy it as much, but it will make you feel better. Paint a smile on your face when you go out.

Then, one day you will awaken, and notice that the sun is shining once again.

> "Healing takes courage, and we all have courage, even if we have to dig a little to find it."
>
> ~Tori Amos

MY ACTION PLAN for HEALING AFTER A BREAK-UP:

I is for INTIMACY

"Live with passion and compassion, proceed with optimism, value disciplined thinking, be open to intimacy and love the mystery."
~Peter Swift

Are you comfortable with intimacy?

Intimacy has sometimes been referred to as *Into-Me-See*. That makes some people uncomfortable. How about you? How can you deepen the intimacy with someone you're dating and discover their intimate selves?

Step 1: Have fun together.
Of course, if you're together, you're already doing this. You need to keep doing it.

Doing things together that are fun for both of you is absolutely essential to deepened intimacy. There's no substitute for shared time.

Step 2: Do boring stuff together.
All couples go on dates in the beginning, but you know you're getting intimate when you start sharing grocery trips together.

Intimacy comes with familiarity, knowledge, and mutual reliance. Let each other into the nitty-gritty of your lives.

> *"Among men, sex sometimes results in intimacy, among women, intimacy sometimes results in sex."*
>
> *~Barbara Cartland*

Step 3: Spend time with each other's families.
A lot of people get freaked out when it's time to "meet the parents." This shows good sense.

Getting to know your partner's family is a big step. You'll get to know each other in a much deeper way.

Step 4: Learn your partner's language of love.
When it comes to the expression of love, there are as many languages as there are people.

For you, being told "you look pretty today" makes today your own personal Christmas. For you partner, it's like saying "Good morning"—nice, but not exactly a bolt of electricity.

Learn what makes your partner feel special. Will your partner feel loved if you pick flowers? Buy a special present? Take out the garbage? Do what your partner likes, and respect that you may not like the same things.

> "We have two ears and one mouth so that we can listen twice as much as we speak."
>
> ~Epictetus

Step 5: Practice good listening skills.
Talking and listening take constant practice. It's just not possible for two people to be intimate with each other without some misunderstandings.

Take time for slow conversations. Be a "responsive listener." Verbally assure your partner you're present and listening. Say, "um-hum," "that sounds annoying," or "I'm so glad!"

Don't assume you know what your partner means. Speak back what you hear before you give you own opinion.

Step 6: Talk about your feelings.
I'm not talking about sharing to your beloved that the driver ahead of you is a moron. Talk about things that make you feel vulnerable and sad, things that you secretly hope for, things that you share with no one else.

Talking can be harder than you think.

Step 7: Talk about sex.
I don't mean have sex talk—not that sex talk is a bad idea. What I'm telling you, though, is talk *about* sex.

Talk about what you like. Talk also about what you don't like. Discussing your sex life requires great trust and great intimacy.

Step 8: Create situations for conversations.
Talking is important. You need to talk about your feelings, about what you do together, about your memories, values, and future goals. Not all these conversations just *happen*. Sometimes you have to plan for them.

Reading books together, going to museums and lectures, or volunteering together can make "issues" arise for you to talk about. You'll have a chance to discover similarities and differences.

Alternatively, you can go at it directly. Ask each other over dinner: Do you want children? Do you think spanking kids is okay? What do you think about immigration? If you had a billion dollars, would you give it to charity?

Whatever method you use, try to get to know each other's wider interests and opinions.

> "I will not play tug o' war. I'd rather play hug o' war. Where everyone hugs instead of tugs, Where everyone giggles and rolls on the rug, Where everyone kisses, and everyone grins, and everyone cuddles, and everyone wins."
>
> ~Shel Silverstein

Step 9: Cuddle.
You don't have to cuddle. You can hold hands. The point is, being together physically, and not only in sex, encourages intimacy.

Step 10: Be independent.
To be really intimate with another person, you need to be yourself. Don't get so lost in a relationship that you forget your own interests. Pursuing a career, a hobby, or your own group of friends helps develop a well-rounded self. You can then offer yourself to a deep, intimate relationship.

Remember, no one on the outside can tell you how to get closer inside. You have to know yourself, and you have to know your partner. Luckily, getting to know each other is exactly what will bring you closer.

> "It is not time or opportunity that is to determine intimacy – it is disposition alone. Seven years would be insufficient to make some people acquainted with each other, and seven days are more than enough for some."
>
> ~Jane Austen

MY ACTION PLAN for INTIMACY:

J is for JUST DO IT!

GO OUT AND DATE

"Take action in order to move closer to your goals."
~Les Brown

Let me ask you a question. If you wake-up one year from now and your life and relationships are exactly the same as they are today, will you be happy?

If yes – great – keep doing what you're currently doing.

If not, its time to take action.

Sometimes singles are afraid to ask someone out or afraid to date. I understand, putting oneself "out there" can be scary.

But, you can only read *so many* books and write *so many* dream mate lists before its time to get out and practice!

If you think you're "saving yourself" for the perfect person before you go out on a date, you're confused.

Everyone needs practice, whether you're planting a vegetable garden or riding a bicycle. It's no different with dating.

ABC's OF DATING: Simple Strategies for Dating Success!

> *"If you only do what you know you can do – you never do very much."*
>
> ~Tom Krause

Where will you go to meet eligible singles?

What's your strategy for asking someone out – whether you're a man or a woman?

Where will you go on a date?

How will you know if they're right for you?

Finish reading this book. Go back and re-read the previous chapters in this book if you must – but only once – then *get out there*!

After each date, write down three things you really liked about your date. Are those qualities on your dream mate list? If not, add them.

Also write down three qualities about you date that you didn't like. Now, turn these negative qualities into positive characteristics and add those to your dream mate list too.

Do this exercise every time you date someone.

Maybe you notice your dating skills need work, or you want to be more comfortable flirting. Maybe what you thought was important in a mate isn't as important as something else you just realized.

Go out and date. You need the practice.

MY ACTION PLAN for JUST DO IT! GO OUT AND DATE:

K is for Kindness

"Kindness is the language which the deaf can hear and the blind can see."
~Mark Twain

Are you a kind person?

Kindness is critical in relationships and when dating.

People ultimately fall in love with people who make them feel good.

Humans have the ability to choose behavior in the moment. You can choose to be kind, or mean or indifferent.

The behavior you choose will effect your dates, your relationships and ultimately your life.

Here are some ways to see how kind a person you really are:

- You say "yes" a lot more than "no" when a person asks you for a favor.

- You don't interrupt when someone is talking.

- You routinely look for the good in others.

- Your sense of humor is charming and not biting or sarcastic.

- You are generous.

- You are considerate of others.

- You are helpful and warmhearted.

- You rarely speak unkind words.

- You are polite when speaking to others.

- You listen to others with you head and your heart.

- You share.

- You perform acts of kindness without expected praise from others.

- You compliment others freely.

- You practice living in the moment.

- You value and appreciate other's differences.

- You treat others with respect, including people of "lesser status."

- Your teasing is fun and not hurtful.

Kindness has a powerful circular effect.

Be kind to yourself and to those you date, intentionally and on a regular basis.

Practice random acts of kindness and experience all the joy life has to offer.

> "No act of kindness, no matter how small, is wasted."
>
> ~Aesop

MY ACTION PLAN for KINDNESS:

L is for LISTENING

"The first duty of love is to listen."
~Paul Tillich

What's the most important thing in a relationship? You might say love, you might say trust, you might say passion, but what I think makes a relationship work is *communication*.

You can have common values and chemistry, but if you don't have communication, the relationship is going to get hard-going sooner or later.

Listening is a very important part of communication and critical for couples, whether dating or in a committed relationship.

First: Make time *not* to listen to each other. It may sound strange (and a bit exasperating) but one of the most important things couples need is time for *not talking*.

So much of your time is dedicated to getting things done, with your job, your home, and your relationship.

Make sure you're spending *fun* time together. Your dates don't have to be elaborate. Go out to dinner. Go on a walk or watch a movie. It's so much easier to hear what the other person has to say when you like spending time with that other person.

> *"A wise old owl sat on an oak; The more he saw the less he spoke; The less he spoke the more he heard; Why aren't we like that wise old bird?"*
>
> ~Anonymous

Second: Practice "responsive listening". Respond to what your partner says, even if you have nothing to say. Phrases like, "that sound difficult," "I can see what you mean," and even "um-hum" show your partner that you're engaged.

Third: Don't assume you understand. People are different. We may say the same words but mean different things. Before you respond make sure you understand what was meant.

> *"To listen well, is as powerful a means of influence as to talk well, and is as essential to all true conversations."*
>
> ~Anonymous

Fourth: Be aware of the other person's facial expressions and body language. Nonverbal messages tell you more than a person's words or tone of voice. Understand the hidden messages of your date's / partner's words. Don't know? Just ask.

Fifth: Stay focused. Faking attention, daydreaming, being distracted, or feeling restless and eager to end the conversation are all signs of poor listening habits. Set aside time to listen to your partner and be respectful of what they have to say. You might learn something about them you didn't know.

MY ACTION PLAN for LISTENING:

m is for MATURITY

"Maturity of mind is the capacity to endure uncertainty."
~John Finley

A person's level of maturity is often described as their Emotional Intelligence Quotient (EQ) or, as coined by Daniel Goleman in his book of the same name, Emotional Intelligence.

EQ describes a person's ability to identify, assess and manage their own emotions and the emotions of others.

Are you currently entangled in difficult or dramatic relationships? Do you suffer from old trauma? Are you unable to resolve painful emotions? What is your level of maturity, your EQ?

It's time to take an honest look at oneself. If you're not experiencing the healthy relationships you desire, you will need to make some changes before you attract the life partner you're searching for.

Every relationship you have – past, present and future - is a hologram of your life in that moment.

> *Maturity has more to do with what types of experiences you've had and what you've learned from them, and less to do with how many birthday's you've celebrated.*
>
> *~Unknown*

Ask yourself – honestly – these eight questions:

1. How well do you cope with unexpected change?

2. How able are you to recognize your feelings as they occur?

3. Are you able to express your feelings appropriately.

4. How well do you listen to other people's ideas?

5. How well do you control strong emotions and impulses?

6. Do you take responsibility for your behavior and your actions or do you blame others?

7. Are you able to act with maturity under stress?

8. Do you withdraw from conflict or uncomfortable situations?

> *Are you proud of the way you "show up" in relationships or are you, at times, out of control, avoiding or unable to express your feelings and emotions?*
>
> ~Coach Katherin

Knowing that we can all make improvements in our behaviors, where do you want to change for the better?

> *"To exist is to change, to change is to mature, to mature is to go on creating oneself endlessly."*
>
> ~Henri Bergson

Here is a list of possible areas to work on in order to improve your current and future relationships and therefore, allow you to attract a healthier love relationship.

Learn to:

- Communicate appropriately in each relationship
- Build and maintain friendships
- Understand your emotional "triggers"
- Inspire and lead others
- Actively participate in your community
- Share responsibility
- Clarify assumptions

MY ACTION PLAN for MATURITY:

n is for NON-NEGOTIABLE REQUIREMENTS

"Dating should be less about matching outward circumstances than meeting your inner necessity."
~Unknown

There are certain requirements in a relationship that are absolutely non-negotiable.

Do you know your non-negotiable requirements?

The test for a non-negotiable is that the relationship *will not work for you* if it's missing.

The absence of a single non-negotiable often results in a failed relationship.

A clear example of a common non-negotiable requirement is fidelity. If unmet, the relationship will not work.

Non-negotiables are typically fulfilled or unfulfilled, met or not, black or white. No grey area exists.

Non-negotiable requirements typically involve religion, money, children, lifestyle, goals and values.

An unmet requirement is usually an unsolvable problem and typically results in one of three choices:

1) leave the relationship (most common)
2) let go of the requirement (possible but rare)
3) negotiate the requirement (possible but difficult)

To be clear, if a requirement seems easily negotiable, it is probably a need and will have many possible alternatives to being met in the relationship.

Requirements are a characteristic of your relationship and not traits of your partner.

Below is a **sample list of requirements**. This list is not comprehensive. It is intended to get you started thinking. Your non-negotiable requirements come from your clear vision of the relationship you desire.

> Affectionate
> Alignment with Values and Purpose
> Addiction-Free
> Appreciate Differences
> Authenticity
> Balance of Giving and Receiving
> Caring
> Common Vision/Purpose
> Compassionate
> Curious
> Emotional Intelligence
> Emotional Intimacy
> Empathetic
> Expressive
> Family Oriented
> Financial Responsibility
> Financially Secure

***ABC*'s OF DATING:** Simple Strategies for Dating Success!

Flexibility
Generous
Good Listening
Healthy Mind, Body, Spirit
Honesty
Honor each other's space
Humble
Independence
Integrity
Intelligence
Imaginative
Kindness
Life-Long Learner
Love Animals / Pets
Love Children
Monogamy / Fidelity
Mutual Emotional Support
Mutuality
Negotiate Differences Positively
Organized
Passion
Physically Compatible
Playful
Proactive in Relationship
Respect each other's feelings
Respect each other's opinions
Responsive to Needs
Romance
Sensuality
Shared Domestic Responsibility
Shared Dreams for the Future
Shared Primary Interests
Shared Sense of Adventure
Shared Sense of Humor
Shared Religious / Spiritual Beliefs

Spontaneity
Support for each other's goals
Supportability
Trust
Understanding

What are your top non-negotiable requirements?

Are you willing to walk away from a relationship if you truly believe a non-negotiable requirement is missing?

MY ACTION PLAN for NON-NEGOTIABLE REQUIREMENTS:

ABC's OF DATING: Simple Strategies for Dating Success!

O is for OWNING YOUR OWN ISSUES

"New York is definitely haunted. Old lovers, ex-boyfriends, anyone you have unresolved issues with you are bound to run into again and again until you resolve them."
~Sarah Jessica Parker

Let's start this chapter with two questions.

"What did you do to contribute to the *health* of your last relationship?"

– and –

"What did you do to contribute to the *demise* of your last relationship?"

Every one of us has a healthy way of dealing with our emotions and every one of us has destructive and irrational behaviors.

Our dark side can quickly sabotage a relationship.

Here are four unhealthy behaviors to watch out for, both in yourself and in your partner:

#1 Attack.
When you're irritated or in an argument with your partner do you typically use hurtful words, burst your temper, raise your voice or stare viciously at them?

#2 Blame.
Do you find fault with your partner or make unfair accusations? Do you lack the courage to talk about what's really on your mind and instead criticize your partner or deflect from the real issues?

#3 Acquiesce.
Do you employ passive aggressive behaviors in such an indirect way as to escape accountability for your decisions and behavior? Do you ever consent passively, knowing you will never follow-through with what you promised?

#4 Withdraw.
Do you give up, either emotionally and/or physically withdrawing from an argument or difficult situation with your partner?

These behaviors may allow you to temporarily get your needs met, but your short-term gain will turn to resentment and bitterness in the long-term.

> *"Everyone is ignorant – but on different issues."*
>
> ~Will Rogers

What things trigger you?

What makes you "stuck"?

How do you respond in conflict?

Are you punishing your current relationship for something someone did to you in the past?

By owning your own issues, you're taking responsibility for yourself and not blaming others for your problems or short-falls.

Strive to get better. Clear up your issues now, before they do irrevocable damage to your relationship.

MY ACTION PLAN for OWNING YOUR OWN ISSUES:

P is for Positive Mental Attitude

"A healthy attitude is contagious but don't wait to catch it from others. Be a carrier."
~Unknown

Are you the type of person who lights a candle or the type who curses the darkness?

A Positive Mental Attitude is a psychological term with the central belief that a person can increase their achievement through optimistic thought.

Simply said, change your mindset to see good and you will achieve more success in life.

It's been said that we are the average of the five people we spend time with. People in our lives are a reflection, a mirror, of us.

If you don't like the people you spend time with or the people you currently attract into your life to date, you must change YOU as you are the constant in those relationships.

Easier said than done, right?

> *"What we focus on expands and becomes our reality. Instead of spending time thinking about how bad things are, think about the good things already in your life."*
>
> *- Coach Katherin*

When you dwell on the negative aspects of life or compare your failures to another's success, you may become discouraged or depressed.

Having a Positive Mental Attitude will improve your outlook.

Here are eight steps to take now to retrain your thoughts.

Step 1: Put yourself first
When you constantly try to please others and become the person they want you to be, you cheat yourself out of your own dreams.

What do you want in life? Plan your daily routine to include at least one or two elements that will bring you closer to your goals.

Step 2: Change your self-talk
Self-talk is the internal dialogue we use to view the world, explain situations and communicate to ourselves.

Be aware of how you speak to yourself and change your negative self-talk to be more kind, loving and gentle towards yourself.

Step 3: Ditch the negative people
Remove the negative influences in your life, at least temporarily, until you are strong enough to be a positive influence on them.

Hang out with happy healthy people who represent the kind of people you want to be and learn from them.

> "Are you a SNIOP? Someone who is Sensitive to the Negative Influences Of Others?
>
> ~Zig Ziglar

Step 4: Stay in control
Understand that even if you cannot control outside influences, you can control your reaction to them.

Step 5: Learn to slow down
When constantly pressured by unfinished tasks and deadlines, you can develop a negative attitude towards life.

Become more organized, learn to say "no" more often to unnecessary tasks and let go of unnecessary expectations. Learn to live in the moment more often.

Step 6: Develop and attitude of gratitude
Make a list of positive aspects in your life. List your achievements, your talents, those positive influences in your life and everything you do well.

Read this list when you need a mental boost. Retrain your mind to see what's good in your life – today.

> *"Develop an attitude of gratitude, and give thanks for everything that happens to you, knowing that every step forward is a step toward achieving something bigger and better than your current situation."*
>
> *~Brian Tracy*

Step 7: Be a student
Learn something new every day. Expand you mind with new thoughts and ideas. Take a class, study a new language, or learn a new hobby. You will encourage a positive attitude by providing something new in your life.

> "Lose yourself in generous service and every day can be a most unusual day, a triumphant day, an abundantly rewarding day."
>
> ~William Arthur Ward

Step 8: Be in service
Helping others allows us to be thankful for the blessings in our lives. Make volunteering part of your life.

MY ACTION PLAN for A POSITIVE MENTAL ATTITUDE:

Q is for QUIT THE NEGATIVE RELATIONSHIP PATTERNS

"Of all the stratagems, to know when to quit is the best."
~Chinese Proverb

Do most of your relationships end in a similar way?

Do most of your dates treat you the same?

Does it ever seem that the person you're currently dating is just like the person you used to date?

We've all heard the definition of insanity; doing the same thing over and over again and expecting different results.

What are you doing over and over again in your dating that still isn't getting you the results you want?

Take a few minutes to fill-in the Relationship History exercise that follows. You will begin to recognize patterns – both good and bad – that ultimately affect your future relationships.

Following the exercise are a few questions that will help you realize what relationship habits and patterns are positive and assisting you in a positive way in your life, and which are negative and therefore, have a negative impact on your life and on your dating and relationship experiences.

ABC's OF DATING: Simple Strategies for Dating Success!

Relationship History Exercise:

a) In the space below, write the NAME of 10 people you recently dated. If you haven't dated 10 people lately, its fine to list people you used to date a while ago (or even those you had a crush on in high school).

b) By the "+" list what you appreciated about each relationship and how you benefitted from it.

c) By the "-" list what you didn't like about the relationship or how you might have been hurt by this person.

d) List the REASON you're not currently in relationship with that person (if applicable). List what broke up the relationship or why you no longer see the person.

1. NAME _____
    + _____
    - _____
    REASON _____

2. NAME _____
    + _____
    - _____
    REASON _____

ABC's OF DATING: Simple Strategies for Dating Success!
___

3. NAME _____
   + _____
   - _____
REASON _____

4. NAME _____
   + _____
   - _____
REASON _____

5. NAME _____
   + _____
   - _____
REASON _____

6. NAME _____
   + _____
   - _____
REASON _____

7. NAME _____
   + _____
   - _____
REASON _____

8. NAME _____
   \+ _____
   \- _____
   REASON _____

9. NAME _____
   \+ _____
   \- _____
   REASON _____

10. NAME _____
    \+ _____
    \- _____
    REASON _____

> "A good relationship has a pattern like a dance."
>
> ~Anne Morrow Lindberg

Now let's take a closer look at your **Relationship Patterns.**

a) What positive patterns have been repeated in your relationship?

b) What negative patterns have been repeated?

c) Of the positive patterns, which were your behaviors and which were the behaviors of the other person?

d) Of the negative patterns, which were your behaviors and which were the behaviors of the other person?

e) Of the negative patterns, which do you want to eliminate from your future relationships?

f) Of the negative patterns, which do you want to change in your future relationships?

g) What specific action(s) will you commit to in order to change the negative pattern(s) in your relationships?

h) What are the desired outcomes for committing to making the changes in your relationship patterns?

MY ACTION PLAN for QUIT THE NEGATIVE RELATIONSHIP PATTERNS:

ABC's OF DATING: Simple Strategies for Dating Success!

R is for ROMANTIC REJECTION

"I take rejection as someone blowing a bugle in my ear to wake me up and get going, rather than retreat."
~Sylvester Stallone

Rejection is probably the hardest part of dating. You put yourself out there, show you're interested, even let someone get to know you—and then they turn you down. It's tempting just to stay home.

Here's the thing, though: you can't stay home.

Rejection is tough, but it's tougher to be alone for the rest of your life. You have to risk rejection to find acceptance. So how do you move on?

The first thing you have to realize is **romantic rejection isn't personal**. Well, sometimes it is, and in those cases you should move on to the second lesson.

In the vast majority of cases, your rejection says nothing bad about you. You may be rejected because you're in the wrong place at the wrong time. Women say "it's not a good time" as an excuse, but often it's true.

Or your timing for asking someone out was bad; or the location. (Funerals are bad occasions; generally speaking, so are carwashes.)

You may also be rejected because you just don't fit. I know, he's hot, but face it, you work with horses and he hates animals. That's his problem. Don't make it yours.

Second, **sometimes rejection *is* your fault.** If you go up to a woman, as John Nash did in *A Beautiful Mind,* and say, "I want to have intercourse with you," the odds of a favorable reception are not good.

In those cases, use your rejection as an opportunity to **improve your dating skills.** How are you putting yourself across? What are you doing wrong? Don't whine about your bad luck; be proactive and fix it.

> "There's nothing like rejection to make you do an inventory of yourself."
>
> ~James Lee Burke

Third, **turn to your friends.** People love you. True, you were looking for a different kind of love, but that's no reason to turn your friends away. Your friends know you well. They can see you're loveable and attractive.

Fourth, **take care of yourself.** Whether you're dealing with the rejection of a stranger at a bar or your partner's cheating, you're not going to be helped by taking your feelings out on yourself.

Sleep, eat well, and exercise. I know bodily care is an unromantic response to the tragedies of life, but it really will help. Especially the exercise. And maybe you can meet someone new at the gym.

> *"Reach high, for stars lie hidden in your soul. Dream deep, for every dream precedes the goal."*
>
> *~Pamela Vaull Starr*

Fifth, don't let rejection interfere with your life. Continue to **pursue your goals.** Whether you're single or not, you need to follow your own interests. A partner is no substitute for a self. Also, having a strong, independent life is one of the surest ways to attract a stable partner.

And finally, **eat chocolate.** Be happy! You're not going to move on by moping. Eat gummy bears if you have some freakish aversion to chocolate.

Everyone has been rejected in love. (Let's hope so, anyway. If we have to go through it, everyone should.)

Rejection is just part of the romance game. Move on. Attraction and acceptance are part of the romance game, too.

> "A rejection is nothing more than a necessary step in the pursuit of success."
>
> ~Bo Bennett

MY ACTION PLAN for ROMANTIC REJECTION:

***ABC*'s OF DATING:** *Simple Strategies for Dating Success!*

S is for SUCCESSFUL SINGLE

"I'm single because I was born that way."
~Mae West

There is one single reason - and only one reason - for anyone to have a partner in their life. And that reason is: drum roll please – ADDED VALUE.

A partner is not there to "complete" you or make you happy. They are there to *add value* to your already successful single life.

Are you putting your life on hold waiting for a relationship to happen, for that perfect partner to arrive and make your "whole"?

The best way to find your life partner is to be a happy, confident and successful single person living the life you really want.

> *"I don't need a man to rectify my existence. The most profound relationship we'll ever have is the one with ourselves."*
>
> *~Shirley MacLaine*

Are the following statements true for you or are there emotional issues still hovering which are keeping you from being successfully single?

- I've let go of relationships which are damaging to me.

- My past relationship experiences do not impact my present relationships.

- I've forgiven my parents / guardians for my past and present unmet needs.

- I've forgiven myself for my past mistakes.

- I've forgiven people who have hurt me in the past.

- I trust everyone does the best they can.

- I'm aware of and own my emotional issues and triggers when they arise in a relationship.

- I engage freely in activities and hobbies which bring joy and happiness in my life.

- I currently experience many healthy relationships in my life.

> *"I have never loved another person the way I loved myself."*
>
> ~Mae West

Don't put your life on hold waiting for a relationship to happen. Live your life fully while you're single.

If you're not yet ready for call yourself "successfully single" or aren't yet ready to pursue a committed partnership due to timing (recently divorced), health (physical / mental / or emotional issues), finances or lifestyle, it's best to date a variety of people on a non-exclusive basis and have fun.

Spend the time learning more about yourself and your relationships and become ready for the life and love you really want.

MY ACTION PLAN for SUCCESSFUL SINGLE:

T is for TELL THE TRUTH

"Take advantage of every opportunity to practice your communication skills so that when important occasions arise, you will have the gift, the style, the sharpness, the clarity, and the emotions to affect other people."
~Jim Rohn

How often do you tell your dates the truth?

Always? Most of the time?

Have you ever said "I'll call you," when you really meant "I have no intention of ever talking to you or going out with you again"?

Have you ever told your date you had an appointment or prior engagement when you really meant "I really don't want to spend time with you"?

It's not that we want to lie to the people we're dating.

Sometimes people just don't know how to express themselves or don't know how to say what they're really thinking and feeling.

What if I can teach you a simple, fast and effective way of conversing with anyone in any situation? Imagine how helpful that would be for you!

> *"Love bravely, live bravely, be courageous, there's really nothing to lose."*
>
> ~Jewel

It's called the **Courageous Conversation Model.**

The three steps of this model are:

"I feel..."

"I think..."

"I want..."

Here's an example of how it's used:

Let's say its lunchtime and you're thinking about eating.

Using the Courageous Conversation Model you would say, "I feel hungry. I think it's time for lunch and I want to go next door and eat Chinese food with Mary."

Simple, right? Sure, it's an easy example.

Let's take another, more difficult example about Todd.

Todd was recently divorced and was scheduled to meet Mary, a woman he'd been corresponding with online. They were supposed to meet for coffee at 6pm at the coffee shop close by her work.

At 6:20pm, Todd was still sitting alone waiting for Mary to arrive. They'd exchanged cell phone numbers but Todd didn't want to appear desperate so he didn't call her.

At 6:30pm Todd finished his coffee and got up to leave, just as Mary walked through the door.

Mary introduced herself and simply said, "Sorry I'm late." Todd responded, "That's okay."

Of course it wasn't okay with Todd. He was distracted the entire date thinking about how rude Mary was and how disrespectful he felt because of her tardiness and no explanation.

Todd called me from the parking lot just after he ended the date with Mary, asking for my advice.

I stepped Todd through the Courageous Conversation Model.

What Todd had wanted to say to Mary just after she had arrived was this; "I'm annoyed that you're so late. I thought we were going to meet at 6pm and yet its 6:30pm and you just arrived. I expected you to call if you were going to be late."

He stepped through the model again. "I feel disrespected. I thought you were interested in meeting me in person. I want you to be on time for our dates."

Todd understood the reason he hadn't expressed himself to Mary was because he wasn't feeling confident enough to talk about his emotions.

He also understood he had wasted the entire date distracted by his inability to communicate and hadn't even gotten to know more about Mary.

> *"May you always be courageous, stand upright and be strong."*
>
> ~Bob Dylan

We all need to be more courageous in our conversations with people – especially people we're dating or in relationship with.

Practice expressing yourself using the Courageous Conversation Model. Practice with an easy example first, then practice with a more difficult situation.

One additional point – watch your body language when you're using this model.

If your body language is closed or defensive, or worse, aggressive - take a moment to breathe deeply and relax into a more open body posture.

People are more apt to "hear" you when your body language is open to them.

> "I've learned to trust myself, to listen to truth, to not be afraid of it and to not try and hide it."
>
> ~Sarah McLachlan

MY ACTION PLAN for TELL THE TRUTH:

U is for UNDERSTANDING

MEN & WOMEN

"Tis better to understand, than to be understood."
~Anonymous

Men and women are different. There, I said it.

Dating and relationships would be better if men understood what women want and women more clearly understood what men want.

> *"I know that you believe you understand what you think I said, but I'm not sure you realize that what you heard is not what I meant."*
>
> ~Robert McCloskey

Ladies first!

It's no secret what women want; they want a man who knows what a woman wants. And, they don't want to have to tell him. But just to clarify, here's what women want.

ABC's OF DATING: Simple Strategies for Dating Success!

1. **Attentiveness.**
   Women want to feel special. They want to know a man is paying attention to her. He remembers what she says, remembers important dates, and thinks she's wildly, wonderfully different from any other woman.

2. **Women want a strong emotional connection.**
   Women want deep emotional intimacy with a man. This intimacy is special, unlike any other intimacy she has, with her family or her girlfriends.

   She wants to be open and vulnerable with a man and know he *gets her* and *supports her*. The man doesn't need to be emotional, but he needs to be able to connect with her in an emotional way.

3. **Women want physical attention.**
   Women want good sex. They also want to hold hands, to be kissed for no reason, and to cuddle. Women want to feel beautiful, sexy, and cherished.

   They don't want to feel like a vehicle for a man's sexual pleasure, so it's important to show physical affection when it's not going to lead to sex.

> *"Confidence looks sexy on every body."*
>
> ~Coach Katherin

4. **Women want confidence.**

   Women don't like arrogance. They don't want a man who swaggers and boasts and spouts his accomplishments.

   They do want a man who can take care of himself, who can hold his own with other men, and who won't crumple or turn bitter offered some constructive criticism.

5. **Women want success.**

   Not every woman wants a man who drives a sports car. Most women do want a man who can decide what he wants and does it. If that means making a lot of money, that's fine. If that means devoting your life to vanquishing AIDS in Africa, that's fine, too.

   What's important is that you're the kind of man who does what he sets out to do. A man needs to show drive and initiative—with a woman and with other areas of his life.

6. **Women want respect.**
   A woman wants to be respected by a man. She wants to know her ideas and values are important to him.

   She wants him to treat her well in front of other people and when alone. She also wants to be able to respect her man.

7. **Women want kindness.**
   Women want a man with enough initiative to sweep her off her feet, but they also want a man who is sweet, gentle and kind.

   Women like men who show them and others consideration and thoughtfulness.

8. **Women want love.**
   Women want to be loved. They want to be a man's only woman, someone who can satisfy him, someone who endlessly fascinates him.

   They want a man who lets her know he loves her—over and over and over again, as if he's never told her before.

Women can seem mysterious, but really they're not. They want to be loved, and they want a man worth loving.

> *"Everything that irritates us about others can lead us to an understanding of ourselves."*
>
> ~Carl Gustav Jung

Next, let me clarify for the gentlemen.

What do men really want in a woman? Are they really those sex-crazed creatures we take them for? Yes and no.

There are definitely men out there who aren't looking for a relationship, who just want a hot body to show off and enjoy.

But there are also men who are ready to settle down and commit themselves to a woman. What are they looking for?

1. **Beauty.**
    Let's get that one out of the way. Yes, men want beauty. They want a face that's wonderful to wake up to. That doesn't mean men all want to marry Angelina Jolie. Men do have different standards of beauty. What unites them is a desire and appreciation for beauty.

2. **Sexiness.**
    Just because he's started to grow up doesn't mean he's not interested in sex. Again—luckily—men have different standards for sexiness. You don't need five-foot legs.

3. **Respect.**
   Men like women who know how to show them respect. They like women who don't cut them down in front of other people. They want a woman who can trust him to do what he says he's going to do.

   > *"Correction does much, but encouragement does more."*
   >
   > *~Johann Wolfgang von Goethe*

4. **Encouragement.**
   Yes, even men with robust egos appreciate a little ego-stroking now and then. Give a man encouragement. Tell him he does a good job, that you like being with him, that you're proud he's your man. He'll be proud you're his woman.

5. **Fidelity.**
   Men want a woman who will stand with him. A woman who shows support, even when things are rough, is a woman to be relied on and loved.

6. **Open, Honest Communication.**
   Men don't like to be manipulated. They like a woman who can tell them what they think, what they need, and what they want. They like to have the facts directly and not have to fish for them.

7. **Strength and Confidence.**
   Men want women who can be partners. They like being needed, but they don't want her to be a child. They want a woman who is self-assured and can take care of herself.

8. **Goodness.**
   Men value women who are good people—who are consistently, instinctively kind. They like women who will forgive them and look over their faults. They value women who can be trusted absolutely.

> *"I think the next best thing to solving a problem is finding some humor in it."*
>
> *~Frank A. Clark*

9. **Sense of Humor.**
   At the end of the day, a man wants someone who can make him laugh. He needs someone who can share the hardships of day-to-day life and make things easier.

10. **Adventure in the Bedroom.**
    There aren't many men who dislike being in charge in the bedroom, and there aren't many men who dislike having things switched around now and then. A man likes a woman who can try new things, take initiative, and be a real sexual partner.

11. Space.
A man really appreciates a woman who understands the need for space. No matter how much he loves her, a man is bound to need time away sometimes. He'll need time to be with other men, to be alone, or just to be. Unscripted, unneeded, uncensored. Men value (and respect) women who understand this.

12. Challenge.
Men like women who challenge them. They want a woman who makes them want to be a better person, or provide better, or succeed in their career. A man likes to be with a woman who makes him be a man.

13. Love.
Finally, what a man really wants is a woman who loves him. There is nothing like being someone's one and only.

Beauty, sexiness, confidence, humor – yes, they are all important. However, what men ultimately want is to belong with another person... who happens to be exciting in more ways than one.

MY ACTION PLAN for UNDERSTANDING MEN & WOMEN:

ABC's OF DATING: Simple Strategies for Dating Success!

V is for Dating Venues

"Some places speak distinctly. Certain dank gardens cry aloud for a murder; certain old houses demand to be haunted; certain coasts are set apart for shipwrecks."
~Robert Louis Stevenson

As a dating coach, I'm often asked, "Where is a good place to meet like-minded singles." Great question!

Understand however, it's not the place that's most important. You can find a potential partner just about anywhere.

In fact, I bet, any place you can think of, you will find a couple who met there, no matter how bizarre the venue – a funeral, a car accident, during a lightening storm - to name just a few.

However, it's best to increase your chances by spending time at venues where people share more of you values, beliefs and interests.

Outlined below are four levels of dating venues.

Figure out what you're most interested in / passionate about and spend time in those venues getting to know like-minded singles. You will increase your chances significantly of finding a good match for you!

Level 1 Venues: Public Places.
Anybody could be in these places – all ages and all walks of life. The likelihood of meeting your life partner is very minimal, though possible.

Level 1 Examples: beach, coffee shop, concert, convention, festival/fair, grocery store, park, post office, shopping mall.

Something to think about: Brainstorm a list of public places you regularly spend time at. Are you friendly? Do you try to connect with people? Do you always "put your best foot forward" there?

Level 2 Venues: Generic Singles Settings.
You increase your odds of meeting your life partner in these types of settings. However, all you know is that everyone is single (hopefully). Finding qualified, potential partners can be a challenge.

Level 2 Examples: internet dating, introduction agencies, personal ads, singles clubs, singles dances, speed dating events.

Something to think about: Brainstorm a list of the singles settings in your area and on the internet. Do they seem to attract the kind of people you want to get to know? If so, choose to spend time there. If not, eliminate these settings from your list.

Level 3 Venues: Special Interest Settings.
You immediately have something in common with everyone in these settings. They are great places to make new friends, expand your community and have people hook you up with other singles.

Level 3 Examples: charity ball, classes, coffee shops in bookstores, comedy club, company picnics, dog park, friend's wedding, gym, professional networking associations, real estate groups, sporting clubs (cycling, hiking, mountain climbing, rollerblading, skiing, surfing, yachting, etc.), targeted internet dating sites, trade shows, workshops.

Something to think about: List your interests and hobbies and research the settings that offer them, such as classes or clubs. Then sign-up and participate.

Level 4 Venues: Shared Important Goals / Values / Passions
In these settings, you not only have one or more interests in common, you most likely share important values, a common life purpose, lifestyle and community. Level 4 venues are the BEST for finding your life partner!

Level 4 Examples: cash flow game events, church (especially church singles groups), entrepreneurial functions, ethnic potlucks, foreign language groups, personal growth workshops, religious / spiritual groups, service clubs, special dance groups, sporting groups, Toastmasters, travel / adventure clubs, volunteer organizations.

Something to think about: List the communities you're a member of and actively participate in them. List the communities you might have heard of, but haven't yet visited and get involved. Research to find new communities that attract you and spend the time to check them out.

Take note: it's always more productive to become part of the *welcoming committee* than the *clean-up committee*. You will meet more people and have more time to get to know them.

And, if you can't find what you're looking for, consider finding some like-minded singles and start you own group!

Ultimately, to increase your chances of meeting your ideal life partner, expand your support system and network by spending more time in your Level 3 and Level 4 venues. Join communities that align with you interests and values.

MY ACTION PLAN for DATING VENUES:

W is for WILLINGNESS TO WORK

"Love doesn't just sit there, like a stone; it has to be made like bread, remade all the time, made new."
~Ursula Le Guin

Relationships are like plants. The living, growing kind, not those made out of silk or plastic.

And just like plants, relationships need attention and nurturing, aka work.

In order to keep a plant healthy and alive, you need to water it, give it sunshine and good soil and feed it regularly.

A healthy relationship needs regular attention too.

> *"We've got this gift of love, but love is like a precious plant. You can't just accept it and leave it in the cupboard or just think it's going to get on by itself. You've got to keep watering it. You've really got to look after it and nurture it.*
>
> *- John Lennon*

And, a healthy and fulfilling relationship is most always self-work.

Rather than expecting a relationship to make your happy, choose to learn and grow from the challenges and opportunities a relationship creates for you.

"Show-up" fully in your relationship by focusing on the following:

- Heal your emotional baggage

- Understand what triggers you and manage your reactions

- Live consciously in your daily life

- Learn to respond maturely to life's challenges

- Push beyond your comfort zone

- Learn to be vulnerable and lower your defenses

- Manage your fears

- Increase your capacity to love and be loved

- Let go of your need to control your environment and others

- Let go of the past

- Learn to respect and value others

- Become the man or woman you really want to be

***ABC*'s OF DATING: Simple Strategies for Dating Success!**

> *"Love is the ability and willingness to allow those you care for to be what they choose for themselves without any insistence that they satisfy you."*
>
> *~Wayne Dyer*

MY ACTION PLAN for WILLINGNESS TO WORK:

X is for HOW TO eXIT A BAD DATE

"I can't go on any more bad dates. I would rather be home alone than out with some guy who sells socks on the internet."
~Cynthia Nixon

If you've been on a date, you've probably been on a bad one.

Bad dates make for funny stories. There's that episode on *Friends* where Phoebe's date tells her he writes "erotic novels for children," that her breasts are gorgeous, and that he has a PHD (not PhD), all within the first five minutes. Phoebe just got up and left.

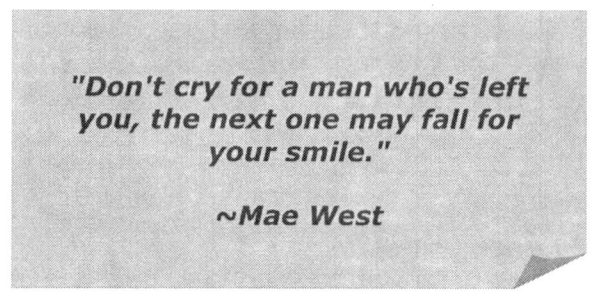

> *"Don't cry for a man who's left you, the next one may fall for your smile."*
>
> *~Mae West*

For a truly rude date, walking out is appropriate. For those poor fools who can't be interesting for more than two minutes at a time, you may need to have a different exit strategy.

Fake a phone call.
You have a number of options here. You can have a friend call you a half-hour into a date.

If it's a bad date, pretend something's happened that makes you need to leave. If it's a good date, just say hi, you're on a date, you'll talk later.

Or you can just fake a phone call. Be careful, though—make sure your ringer and vibrator are turned off. If you're in the middle of a "conversation" and then you're phone rings, you'll be caught.

Alternatively, you can hire Virgin Mobile (or some other service) to be your "friend." Send a text message to Virgin Mobile's "Rescue Ring" service and they'll call you back with an exit.

> "It's my belief we developed language because of our deep inner need to complain."
>
> ~Lilly Tomlin

Complain about work.
Who's going to think you don't, in fact, have too much to do? Well, they might, but who wants to be on a date with someone who's complaining about work?

Fake an illness.
You suddenly have a migraine. You suddenly have a stomach ache. You suddenly have that mysterious marauder, "feminine problems."

Don't pretend to be sick with anything really horrible and make sure you can carry off the lie. (Don't let them see you out dancing in a bar an hour later, though.)

Be a bad date.
Do all the things you're not supposed to do in a date.

Whine. Be rude. Talk about your ex. Or just say things about yourself that will make you undesirable. You're controlling (or too loose). You're messy (or too clean).

Make your date be the one to make a run for the exit.

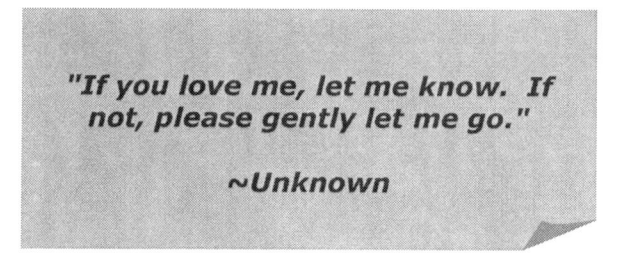

> *"If you love me, let me know. If not, please gently let me go."*
>
> *~Unknown*

Tell the truth.
Chances are good that your date will be honest back.

Chances are also good that their honesty won't be pleasant. Oh, well. At least you'll be out of the date.

Go out the fire escape.
This isn't really graceful, and you probably shouldn't use it to get out of a date with a nice, boring person. But if your date isn't going to take your leaving well, or just doesn't get your subtler clues, climb out the window, go out the door, or lie your way outside.

Take the tried and true approach.
Just tell them you've enjoyed talking with them but they don't seem like a good match for you. Don't give details. Just smile, get up and leave.

And hang in there. For every hundred bad dates, there will be definitely be good ones too.

MY ACTION PLAN for HOW TO eXIT A BAD DATE:

U is for TAKE GOOD CARE OF YOU

"The more care you put into your life, the more life will care for you, bringing you fun adventures, great friends, and real inner security. Caring is just good street-sense."
~Doc Childre

As modern singles, we're a walking tightrope, barely able to balance our daily demands and pressures with the needs of others.

I'm sure you're familiar with the analogy of the airplane oxygen mask. In case of emergency, you're instructed to put the oxygen mask on yourself before helping others.

The same applies in our daily lives, as we can't take care of others if we're on the verge of collapse from lack of self-care.

> *"The name of the game is taking care of yourself, because you're going to live long enough to wish you had."*
>
> ~Grace Mirabella

ABC's OF DATING: Simple Strategies for Dating Success!

90% of Americans report feeling high levels of stress at least once a week.

Physical symptoms of stress include headaches, sleep difficulties and a racing heart.

Emotional signs of stress include crying, edginess, boredom, nervousness, anxiety, overwhelming sense of pressure and being easily upset.

Stress also causes behavioral symptoms such as bossiness, grinding of teeth, inability to get things done, overuse of alcohol and prescription drugs and compulsive eating.

Our thoughts are also affected by stress and manifest in forgetfulness, trouble thinking clearly and constant worry.

Sound familiar?

> *"The life of inner peace, being harmonious and without stress is the easiest type of existence."*
>
> ~Norman Vincent Peale

You need to learn to pamper yourself on a daily basis.

You deserve it.

Here are eight self-care techniques you can do every day to relieve stress and boost your energy.

#1 Keep a stress log.
Every day, write down the events or situations that put you over the edge. Maybe it's your rush-hour drive to work, an irritating noise or talking with a particularly negative person.

Come up with creative ways to eliminate, or at least reduce these triggers in your day.

> *"I'm really into my running workout. Running really helps me clear my head and makes me feel good, especially when I'm stressed."*
>
> *~Katie Holmes*

#2 Exercise
Most people know that exercise boosts energy and relieves stress. You may not know, however, that exercise also increases the cellular production of adenosine triphosphate (ATP), chemical energy produced inside cells. ATP is necessary in every physical activity we do from beating of our heart to running to catch a train.

Make exercise fun. Vary what you do on a daily basis and get a physical trainer to help you create multiple routines to keep you motivated.

#3 Get plenty of rest
Lack of sleep causes weight gain, depression, wrinkles and a short temper. All of these side effects are harmful to dating and relationships!

Aim for sleeping eight hours a day, but never let yourself get more than six.

Not sleeping well? Make sure you have a good mattress, 100% cotton sheets, a new pillow (it's amazing how much a new pillow will enhance your sleep), and a room sufficiently dark and quiet for sleeping.

#4 Deep breathing
Practice "four square breathing":
Inhale slowly to the count of four, hold for the count of four, exhale slowly and completely to the count of four, and hold for the count of four. Repeat four more times.

People who learn to breathe deeply throughout the day have a slower pulse, lower blood pressure and lower levels of cortisol, the primary stress hormone.

#5 Eat balanced meals
Studies have shown American adults are deficient in minerals and vitamins. These deficiencies may not be severe enough to cause disease but they can impair the body's ability to manufacture useable forms of energy.

> *"Water is life's matter and matrix, mother and medium. There is no life without water.*
>
> *~Albert Szent-Gorgyi*

#6 Drink water

Dehydration can result in a range of symptoms, from mild to alarming. Here are a few effects of dehydration:

- dry skin
- dry mouth
- fatigue
- chills
- head rushes
- increased heart rate
- increased respiration
- muscle cramps
- headaches
- nausea
- confusion

Water supports the body's ability to eliminate cell damaging molecules and other toxins that impair energy production.

Drink at least six to eight glasses of water every day.

> "Peak performers use the skill of mental rehearsal of visualization. They mentally run through important events before they happen."
>
> ~Charles Garfield

#7 Visualization

Creative visualization is the technique of using your imagination to create what you want in your life.

Visualize your perfect relationship, health, self-expression, joy, rewarding work, prosperity, inner peace and harmony – whatever your heart desires.

Spend time each day visualizing your perfect life as if it were already so. Chances are good that you will find your life shifting positively in a short time.

#8 Look into the mirror

It may not be a fun exercise for you, but it's important. Closely examine what you see.

How long has it been since you've done something special for yourself?

What can you do to pamper yourself today? Get a haircut, a manicure, a massage. Put on sunscreen, update your wardrobe.

Realize, deep down inside, that you deserve love and a great life. Practice these eight techniques every day. You are worth it and your partner will definitely thank you.

> "Health is the condition of wisdom, and the sign is cheerfulness, an open and noble temper."
>
> ~Ralph Waldo Emerson

MY ACTION PLAN for TAKE GOOD CARE OF YOU:

ABC's OF DATING: Simple Strategies for Dating Success!

Z is for ZOOS and OTHER GREAT PLACES TO DATE

"Someone told me it's all happening at the zoo."
~Paul Simon

Singles are constantly looking for fun and/or romantic date ideas. Whether you just met someone you'd like to get to know better or you've been dating that special someone for a while, it's good to have a list of fun places and things to enjoy with your date.

The **zoo** is a great place to go on a date.

I bet you're not aware of a very special day to visit the zoo? It's November 1st each year. Why? Because, the day after Halloween is the day the zoo keepers feed the larger zoo animals the Halloween pumpkins! Be sure to go at feeding time and watch the frenzy of happy animals get their fill of yummy pumpkins.

Zoos are also a beautiful place to go with your someone special during the Christmas holidays as most zoos' light up their grounds with holiday lights in fun shapes and stay open after dark.

Want other date ideas? Read on.

> *"Fun is good."*
>
> ~Dr. Seuss

Flying kites is fun! Dating should be fun and what's more fun than flying kites together?

Carry two kites in your car – a Barbie kite for her and an Incredible Hulk kite for him! Buy the inexpensive kites at your local dollar store. The purpose is to get to know one another and have fun, not a competition.

Pack a picnic and go to a neighborhood park or somewhere romantic. You can even lay out a blanket in front of the fireplace in your living room and enjoy a special meal together.

Try out a few rounds of **miniature golf**. Getting silly on a mini-golf course can be a great date, no matter how long you have known each other. A new spin on miniature golf is **Frisbee golf**! Never a dull moment with this activity.

Have a **bonfire** on the beach or in a fire pit in the backyard. Roast marshmallows, make s'mores and sing old camp songs. If the weather isn't cooperating, move inside to the living room and use the fireplace.

Take your date to a **comedy club**. There's nothing better than spending time side by side laughing until your sides hurt with someone you want to get to know better.

> *"My advice to you is not to inquire why or whither, but just enjoy your ice cream while it's on your plate."*
>
> *~Thornton Wilder*

Go for **ice cream**, either at the end of a date or just for a quick get-to-know-you outing.

A **concert** is always a fun way to spend time together. There are so many options and depending on the season, there may also be some free concerts in the park or on the beach. Be careful to choose the type of music you would both enjoy.

Fishing has made a dramatic comeback! It's inexpensive, fun and provides an atmosphere conducive to relaxed conversation. Just find a nearby lake or stream.

Boating is another great fun date idea. Just make sure your date doesn't get seasick. You can rent a boat or even go out with a fishing crew for more adventure.

> "I have long thought that anyone who does not regularly – or ever – gaze up and see the wonder and glory of a dark night sky filled with countless stars loses a sense of their fundamental connectedness to the universe."
>
> ~Brian Greene

Spend time with your date **star gazing**. Drive somewhere dark and enjoy the stars. Take an astrology book with you to help you identify the star constellations. Look online to find out what's going on in the stars the night you plan to view them.

Flea Markets are also a fun way to spend time with your date. Do you collect something? Have your date help scour the booths for a lucky find.

The first time I went to a **dinner theatre**, I couldn't believe that someone had actually brought two of my favorite things together – eating and theatre! I especially love those shows that involve the audience. After attending, you and your date will have a lot to talk about for many evenings to come.

Dinner cruises are also a great combination for a fun date. Many cities have them, even if they aren't located on the coast. However, if you ever have a chance to take a dinner cruise around a tropical island with your special someone, it will truly be an evening to remember.

ABC's OF DATING: Simple Strategies for Dating Success!

Taking an **art class** together can lead to a fun, creative and even silly date. Really let go and construct a masterpiece. **Painting unglazed pottery** is an inexpensive and fun way to show your artistic side. Research your local newspaper for painting/pottery shops which host adult nights of margarita and painting specials!

Who doesn't enjoy **bowling**? Many bowling allies have nighttime adult-only bowling. If you haven't been lately, you must go as bowling allies have really changed their atmosphere and have added hip music, strobe and disco lights, good food and beverages, and smoke-free environments. And, if you're not a very good bowler, ask for bumpers! Hey, it's about having fun and enjoying your date, not the strikes.

> "A day hike can be a fantastic way for people to reconnect with the natural world."
>
> ~Gregory Miller

Go on a hike with your date. **Hiking** is an enjoyable activity for two. Plus, you're outside in nature and exercising together – great for active people.

For very adventurous people, I recommend **indoor skydiving** or a **hot air balloon ride** or a **helicopter ride** around your city. Of course, these are more expensive dates, but certainly dates to remember.

Also for the adventurous and young at heart are **amusement parks**. Who can resist being a kid again and enjoying everything from the spinning teacups to the thriller rides?

> *"Dance is the hidden language of the soul of the body."*
>
> ~Martha Graham

Taking **dance lessons** together is a sexy and fun romantic date. My favorites are salsa and swing lessons. A sensual environment plus the physical body contact make this a wonderful date idea.

Have you ever wanted to **rent a sports car** and take a drive with your date? Bring along your favorite tunes and enjoy the ride together.

Ice skating, roller skating or **roller blading** are fun and exciting date ideas. Most places rent skates for a reasonable fee and have places to sit and talk when you're ready to take a break.

Still not enough? Here is a list of other great date ideas:

watching the sunset together
lunch dates
museums
walks in the park
bike ride
local art walks and art gallery showings

weekend street fairs
car shows
visit antique shops
local classes and social events (palm reading classes!)
ferry rides
working out at the gym together
book stores
sporting events
renting a rowboat
indoor rock climbing
getting pampered with side-by-side massage tables
go-carting (both indoor and outside)
going to a casino show
batting cages
a limo ride through the city
wine tasting
cooking classes

and always a tried-and-true favorite – a picnic in the park on a sunny afternoon.

MY ACTION PLAN for ZOOS AND OTHER GREAT PLACES TO DATE:

Afterward

I encourage you to practice the techniques and strategies presented to you in this book. Only with practice will you achieve the results you seek.

Not every technique will be right for you. And not every person will want to achieve the same results.

However, with the strategies and tools presented to you, you have the opportunity to redesign your life and realize the love and outcome you desire.

And remember to have fun along the way.

How many years have you been dating without the results you want? Take action now and find the love you wish for.

It's you life. You deserve the love and life of your dreams!

About the Author

"ABC's of Dating: Simple Strategies for Dating Success!" is Katherin Scott's first book in the **ABC** book series.

Stay tuned for her upcoming books:

ABC's of Online Dating

ABC's of Relationships

ABC's of Attracting Love with Feng Shui

ABC's of Successful Public Speaking

ABC's of Customer Service

and more.

Katherin provides individual dating coaching and couple's relationship coaching by phone, via email or in-person.

As a Certified Feng Shui Consultant, Katherin is available for feng shui consultations, both residential and commercial, which can also be completed over the phone or in-person.

Katherin is also available for private and public speaking events. She is a National Speaker's Association member, trainer and keynote speaker who has a way of capturing her audiences with her wit, inspiration and practical strategies for easy application.

To access free downloads, articles, and Coach Katherin's ezine, and for contact information, visit her website

http://www.KatherinScott.com

2773593

Made in the USA